FSC MIX
Paper from responsible sources
FSC® C001701

We chose to print this title on paper certified by The Forest Stewardship Council® (FSC®), a global, not-for-profit organization dedicated to the promotion of responsible forest management worldwide.

Printed in China

Groundswell Books
Book Publishing Company
PO Box 99, Summertown, TN 38483
888-260-8458
bookpubco.com

ISBN: 978-1-939053-46-6

27 26 25 24 23 22   1 2 3 4 5 6 7 8 9

To my sons, Tiger and Murtagh;
to my daughter, Lilliolani;
and to my grandchildren, Gemma and Tommy.

PAUL

To my four children:
Henrietta, Alexander, Alice, and Charlie,
with love.

SARAH

What is the ocean?

Is the ocean the same as the sea?
Or is it more than the sea?

The ocean is the planet.

The ocean's water is always
moving from place to place
and often changes shape.

It is in the clouds above us.

It is frozen in ice and snow.

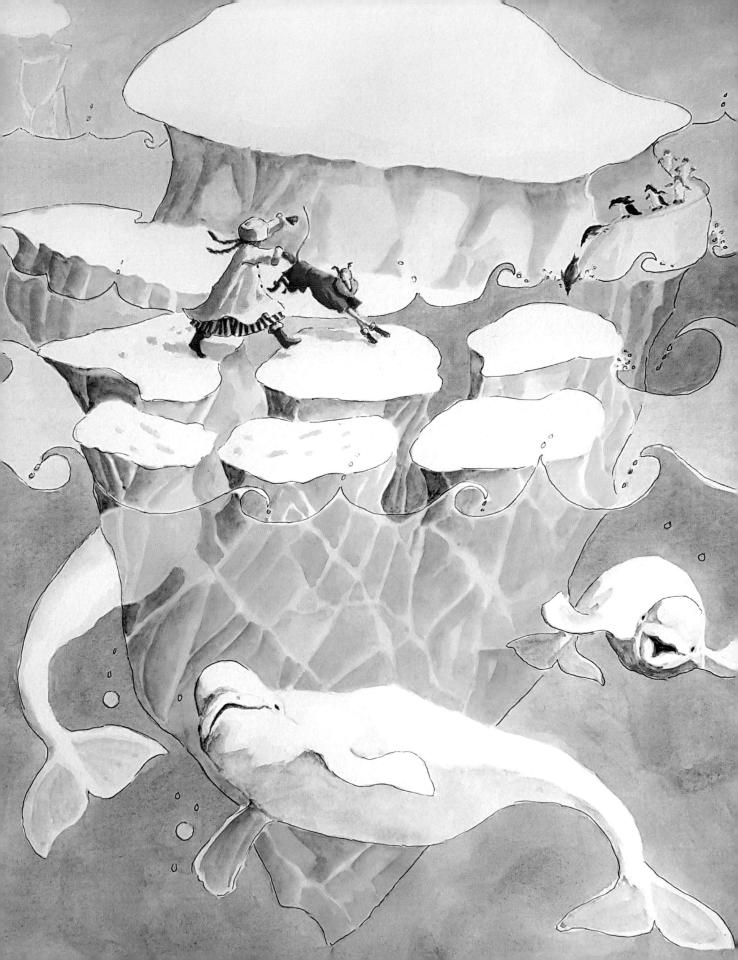

It flows in the ground below us.

It forms our rivers and lakes.

And water from our rivers
flows back into the sea.

Water is in the cells of all
living plants and animals.

This means that the ocean
is inside all living things.

And that means the ocean
is inside you!

The ocean's water is in
your body right now.

The water in your body
was once flowing
in the ground below us.

The water in your body was
once in the clouds above us.

The water in your body was
once frozen in ice and snow.

The water in your body was
once in the bodies of dinosaurs.

All living things
need the ocean's water.

Water is life.

We are made of water.

You are made of water.

We are the ocean!